"As a physician and medical educator, I've seen patients and medical students struggle with the issues addressed in this book. Wayne Grudem's work presents a perfect blend of ethical, moral, technical, and biblical approaches to these critical topics. It will provide understandable guidance for health-care professionals as well as the general public."

Jacqueline Chadwick, MD, family physician; medical educator

"Psalm 119:105 reminds us that God's word is a 'lamp to my feet and a light to my path.' In characteristic fashion, Wayne Grudem has thoroughly applied the word of God to many of the reproductive technologies available today. This book can be a lamp that brightens the path of many couples struggling with the physical and emotional pain of infertility. At the same time, it will illuminate an ethical pathway through the maze of reproductive-technological choices that health-care providers face every day as we counsel our patients."

M. Lance Holemon, MD, board certified
obstetrician-gynecologist

What the Bible Says about Birth Control, Infertility, Reproductive Technology, and Adoption

Books in This Series

What the Bible Says about Abortion, Euthanasia, and End-of-Life Medical Issues

What the Bible Says about Birth Control, Infertility, Reproductive Technology, and Adoption

What the Bible Says about Divorce and Remarriage

What the Bible Says about How to Know God's Will

What the Bible Says about Birth Control, Infertility, Reproductive Technology, and Adoption

Wayne Grudem

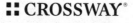
CROSSWAY®

WHEATON, ILLINOIS

What the Bible Says about Birth Control, Infertility, Reproductive Technology, and Adoption

---

Library of Congress Cataloging-in-Publication Data

Names: Grudem, Wayne A., author.
Title: What the Bible says about birth control, infertility, reproductive technology, and adoption / Wayne Grudem.
Description: Wheaton, Illinois: Crossway [2021] | Includes bibliographical references and index.
Identifiers: LCCN 2020014775 (print) | LCCN 2020014776 (ebook) | ISBN 9781433569869 (trade paperback) | ISBN 9781433569890 (epub) | ISBN 9781433569876 (pdf) | ISBN 9781433569883 (mobipocket)
Subjects: LCSH: Birth control—Religious aspects—Christianity. | Birth Control—Biblical teaching. | Human reproductive technology—Religious Aspects—Christianity. | Human reproductive technology—Biblical teaching. | Adoption—Religious aspects—Christianity. | Adoption—Biblical teaching.
Classification: LCC HQ766.25 .G78 2021 (print) | LCC HQ766.25 (ebook) | DDC 241/.663—dc23
LC record available at https://lccn.loc.gov/2020014775
LC ebook record available at https://lccn.loc.gov/2020014776

Crossway is a publishing ministry of Good News Publishers.

BP   29   28   27   26   25   24   23   22   21
14   13   12   11   10   9   8   7   6   5   4   3   2   1

Contents

Introduction...9

PART 1: BIRTH CONTROL

Scripture Views Children Not as a Burden but as a Great
    Blessing 12

Objection: "The World Already Has Too Many People"....17

Birth Control for a Limited Time Is Morally Permissible....20

Morally Acceptable and Morally Unacceptable Methods
    of Birth Control 22

Husbands Should Be Careful Not to Deny to Their Wives
    for Too Long the Privilege and Joy of Having Children...24

An Alternative Viewpoint: All Birth Control is Wrong
    (or All "Artificial" Birth Control Is Wrong)...........25

How Can a Couple Know How Many Children
    to Have? 34

PART 2: INFERTILITY AND
REPRODUCTIVE TECHNOLOGY

Infertility 37

Three Moral Principles to Consider in Relation to
    Reproductive Technology..................................41

Some Modern Reproductive Technologies Are Morally
    Acceptable 46

Other Modern Reproductive Technologies Are Morally
    Unacceptable 59

PART 3: ADOPTION

Adoption 70

FURTHER RESOURCES

Questions for Personal Application 72

Special Terms 73

Bibliography 74

Scripture Memory Passages 77

Hymns 77

Scripture Versions Cited 81

General Index 83

Scripture Index 87

INTRODUCTION

Should we think that birth control is morally acceptable?

If so, are there types of birth control that are morally wrong?

What birth-control methods are morally acceptable?

How do biblical principles help us evaluate modern reproductive technologies, particularly artificial insemination, in vitro fertilization, embryo adoption, and surrogate motherhood?

Why does the Bible view adoption so positively?

This book discusses topics that are related to the conception of children. According to the teachings of the Bible, is it ever right to prevent a woman from conceiving a child? (This is the question of birth control.) On the other hand, what does the Bible teach about couples who are apparently unable to have children? (This is the question of infertility.) And is it right to use modern medical means such as in vitro fertilization, artificial insemination, and even surrogate motherhood to enable a couple to have a baby? (This is the question of modern reproductive technology.)

Finally, what are the teachings of the Bible about a different method of welcoming a child into a family—namely, adoption? As we shall see, there are important principles in Scripture relating to each of these questions.

PART 1: BIRTH CONTROL

Every married couple must face the question of birth control today, and modern society presents a wide variety of viewpoints. On the one hand, many in modern society find no moral problem with birth control, and use condoms and/or birth-control pills commonly in order to have sex while avoiding the fear of unwanted pregnancy.

On the other hand, the Roman Catholic Church considers all forms of birth control to be morally wrong except periodically abstaining from intercourse during a woman's fertile period each month (which is a "natural" as opposed to "artificial" form of birth control).

The *Catechism of the Catholic Church* says:

Unity, indissolubility, and *openness to fertility* are essential to marriage. . . . The refusal of fertility turns married life away from its "supreme gift," the child.[1]

It is necessary that each and every marriage act remain ordered *per se* to the procreation of human life.[2]

Every action which . . . proposes to render procreation impossible is intrinsically evil.[3]

---

1. *Catechism of the Catholic Church*, 2nd ed. (New York: Doubleday, 1997), para. 1664 (463), emphasis added.
2. *Catechism of the Catholic Church*, para. 2366 (628).
3. *Catechism of the Catholic Church*, para. 2370 (629).

Sacred Scripture and the Church's traditional practice see in *large families* a sign of God's blessing and the parents' generosity.[4]

Among evangelical Protestants, a few support essentially the Roman Catholic position and oppose all forms of "artificial" birth control, but most believe that birth control is a personal decision for each family and that couples should be free to decide how many children they will have.

What does the Bible actually teach about birth control? That is the subject discussed in this section.

A. SCRIPTURE VIEWS CHILDREN NOT AS A BURDEN BUT AS A GREAT BLESSING

Some in contemporary society view children mostly as a burden, a huge expense, and an inconvenience that interferes with the happiness of a married couple. From time to time there are news stories that make the task of raising children seem frightfully expensive! In 2013, the U.S. Department of Agriculture estimated that the cost of raising a child from birth to high school graduation was $245,340. In more expensive areas, such as the Northeast United States, that figure reaches $455,000.

That does not include the costs for the college years, which were conservatively estimated by the College Board for 2016–2017 to be $20,090 (in-state) per year for tuition

---

4. *Catechism of the Catholic Church*, para. 2373 (630), emphasis in original.

and housing at four-year public colleges and universities, and $45,370 for four-year private colleges and universities.[5]

But the Bible does not view raising children as a burden or as something that is financially or emotionally impossible to do. It consistently views children as a blessing from God. This positive perspective begins at the earliest point of human history, for the first command that God ever gave to human beings was a mandate to bear children:

> And God blessed them. And God said to them, *"Be fruitful and multiply* and fill the earth and subdue it, and have dominion over the fish of the sea and over the birds of the heavens and over every living thing that moves on the earth." (Gen. 1:28)

To "multiply" implies having more than two children, because a couple with only two children will simply replace themselves on the earth, without multiplying the population.[6]

Other passages in the Old Testament continue promoting a positive view of children, even after Adam and Eve sinned:

> Behold, *children are a heritage from the* LORD,
>   *the fruit of the womb a reward.*
> Like arrows in the hand of a warrior

---

5. "Expenditures on Children by Families, 2015," United States Department of Agriculture, revised March 2017, 20, https://fns-prod.azureedge.net/sites/default/files/crc2015_March2017.pdf. The exact figures are $9,650 per year for in-state public college and university tuition, plus $10,440 for room and board; for private colleges and universities, it is $33,480 for tuition, plus $11,890 for room and board.

6. See below, pp. 17–20, on the question of overpopulation today.

> are the children of one's youth.
> Blessed is the man
> > who fills his quiver with them!
> He shall not be put to shame
> > when he speaks with his enemies in the gate.
> > > (Ps. 127:3–5)

> Your wife will be *like a fruitful vine*
> > within your house;
> your children will be like olive shoots
> > around your table.
> Behold, *thus shall the man be blessed*
> > who fears the LORD. (Ps. 128:3–4)

> Did he not make them one, with a portion of the Spirit in their union? *And what was the one God seeking? Godly offspring.* So guard yourselves in your spirit, and let none of you be faithless to the wife of your youth. (Mal. 2:15)

In the New Testament, Jesus demonstrated a remarkably positive attitude toward children:

> Then children were brought to him that he might lay his hands on them and pray. The disciples rebuked the people, but Jesus said, "Let the little children come to me and do not hinder them, for to such belongs the kingdom of heaven." And he laid his hands on them and went away. (Matt. 19:13–15)

In addition, Paul's directions to Timothy about how he should teach churches included this statement about widows:

> So I would have younger widows marry, *bear children*, manage their households, and give the adversary no occasion for slander. (1 Tim. 5:14)

These passages indicate that the first question couples should ask themselves when considering birth control is this: *Do we agree in our hearts with the Bible's positive view of children as a blessing from God*, or do we agree with a modern secular view that children are an inconvenience and a burden?

This question is important because the Bible is unquestionably prochild in its perspective. The scriptural emphasis on children as a blessing leads me to think that married couples should, in almost all cases, plan to have children sometime in their marriages.[7] In fact, my personal encouragement to most young couples would be to plan to have several children and to enjoy their large families for their entire lifetimes. (I have seldom if ever met couples who told me, "We had too many children.")

Having several children is also a way of expanding the church. Although God's kingdom on earth in the new covenant age is primarily expanded by having spiritual children (people who are born again), not simply through physical

---

7. The rare exceptions would be cases in which the wife has a medical condition, such as a disability that would make pregnancy prohibitively dangerous, or in which couples are past childbearing age when they marry.

procreation, it remains true that the pattern we see in Scripture is that the children of believers ordinarily become believers themselves.[8] Therefore, having several children is also a way for couples to expand the population of God's people in the world, people who will ultimately glorify him for all eternity.

These biblical truths remind us that our primary emphasis in any discussion of birth control should be on the wonderful privilege, joy, and blessing of having children, in many cases having several of them. Children will usually continue to be a blessing and a joy to parents throughout their lives.

However, Scripture also recognizes that sometimes children can be a cause of great sorrow for their parents. Absalom was a source of tremendous grief to David, from his rebellious attempt to usurp David's throne to his death at the hands of David's general Joab (2 Sam. 13–18). The parable of the prodigal son (Luke 15:11–32) tells of a son who must have caused immense grief to his father. And some verses from Proverbs show an awareness of similar tragedies with rebellious children:

> A wise son makes a glad father,
>> but *a foolish son* is a sorrow to his mother.
>>> (Prov. 10:1)

---

8. See Wayne Grudem, *Systematic Theology: An Introduction to Biblical Doctrine* (Leicester, UK: Inter-Varsity, and Grand Rapids, MI: Zondervan, 1994), 500.

> *A foolish son* is a grief to his father
> and bitterness to her who bore him. (Prov. 17:25;
> see also 19:13; 29:3; Deut. 21:18–21)

Nevertheless, these verses show the exceptions rather than the general case, and the overall perspective of Scripture remains very positive toward children. In addition, we may hope that the prophetic promise of Malachi would yet find a partial or even greater fulfillment in our own lifetimes, so that before the day when the Lord comes in judgment, prodigal sons and daughters will be reconciled with their parents:

> Behold, I will send you Elijah the prophet before the great and awesome day of the LORD comes. And he will turn *the hearts of fathers to their children* and *the hearts of children to their fathers*, lest I come and strike the land with a decree of utter destruction. (Mal. 4:5–6)

B. OBJECTION: "THE WORLD ALREADY HAS TOO MANY PEOPLE"

One objection that may be brought against this positive biblical perspective on having children is the idea that the world already has too many people. Someone might argue that in the time of the Bible, there were not very many people on earth and the encouragement to have more children made sense, but today the world already has so many people that there is a danger of overpopulation.

Two answers may be given to this objection. First, the command to "be fruitful and multiply and fill the earth" (Gen. 1:28) expressed God's purpose that Adam and Eve would fill the earth *with God-glorifying people*, people who would honor, serve, and worship God. It is commonly true that children of believers also become believers, and therefore it is still a morally good activity for Christians to have children and thus fill the earth with more God-glorying people. While there are some exceptions, the vast majority of the children of believers, in general, do much more good than harm to the world during their lifetimes.

The other answer is that the world is far from being overpopulated. The pattern throughout all nations of the world is that, as prosperity increases, people have fewer and fewer children. This is acutely evident now in several countries, most notably Canada, Germany, Hungary, Italy, Japan, Russia, and South Korea, where people have had so few children in recent decades that the population is stable or declining, with fertility rates down to as little as 1.5 children per woman.[9] As of May 2020, according to the U.S. Census Bureau, the population of the world was 7.65 billion.[10] In 2004, the United Nations Department of Economic and Social Affairs Population Division published

---

9. Joseph Chamie, "Global Population of 10 Billion by 2100?—Not So Fast," YaleGlobal Online, Oct. 26, 2011, http://yaleglobal.yale.edu/content/global -population-10-billion-2100-not-so-fast. Chamie is the former director of the UN Population Division.

10. U.S. and World Population Clock, U.S. Census Bureau, http://www.census .gov/popclock/.

a paper stating that it expects population to stabilize at about 9.22 billion sometime around 2075.[11] Other models, done later than 2004, show world population stabilizing at 10.1 billion by 2100 because of declining fertility rates.[12] I've discussed the stabilization of world population at greater length in two other books.[13]

In fact, many of the most densely populated areas of the world are also the most prosperous, such as the Netherlands, the United Kingdom, Germany, and Japan. The population density of Massachusetts today (871 people per square mile) is far greater than the population density of China (375 people per square mile) and not greatly less than the population density of India (1,169 people per square mile)[14] but Massachusetts is, in general, a much more pleasant place to live, with a higher standard of living. The difference is increased prosperity, which enables people to have better living conditions.

Neither is it true that the billions of people on the earth are rapidly depleting the earth's resources, so that we will soon have widespread shortages of various essential resources. I have discussed this more fully in other

---

11. "World Population to 2300," United Nations Department of Economic and Social Affairs Population Division, 2004, 12, https://www.un.org/en/development/desa/population/publications/pdf/trends/WorldPop2300final.pdf.

12. Chamie, "Global Population of 10 Billion by 2100?—Not So Fast."

13. See Wayne Grudem, *Politics—According to the Bible: A Comprehensive Resource for Understanding Modern Political Issues in Light of Scripture* (Grand Rapids, MI: Zondervan, 2010), 333–36; *Christian Ethics: An Introduction to Biblical Moral Reasoning* (Wheaton: Crossway, 2018), 1110–13.

14. See Grudem, *Christian Ethics*, 1110, for these and other statistics on population density.

publications,[15] so I will simply say here that an infinitely wise God created for us an earth that was "very good" (Gen. 1:31) and "he formed it to be inhabited!" (Isa. 45:18).

C. BIRTH CONTROL FOR A LIMITED TIME IS MORALLY PERMISSIBLE

While I believe that, in almost all circumstances, married couples should plan to have children sometime, this does not mean they have a moral obligation to have as many children as they are physically capable of having. The existence of modern birth-control methods gives many options for deciding when to have children and how many.

For example, a newly married couple might decide not to have children for the first few years of their marriage, perhaps until their educational process is complete or until they have more financial stability. In such a case, deciding to postpone having children may be a wise and morally good choice.

After a couple has had some children, one or both spouses will often have a sense that "we should not have any more children," perhaps because "we cannot do a good job of raising more children." This can be a morally good and wise decision, because deciding to have more children means taking on another weighty responsibility, and God wants us to be faithful in that responsibility:

15. Grudem, *Politics—According to the Bible*, 320–86; *Christian Ethics*, 1095–1169 (chap. 41).

> But if anyone does not provide for his relatives, and especially for *members of his household*, he has denied the faith and is worse than an unbeliever. (1 Tim. 5:8)

The specific context of this verse is dealing with the provision of support for widows, but the expression "members of his household" would certainly include one's own children too. Regarding this passage, I think John Feinberg and Paul Feinberg are correct when they say that to provide for "members of his household" a person should provide for "financial, physical, emotional, and spiritual needs."[16] Therefore, it is appropriate for couples to consider whether they are reasonably able to do that with more children than they already have.

In addition, Jesus gives a principle that pertains to undertaking obligations generally, and it can appropriately apply to the question of having more children:

> For which of you, desiring to build a tower, does not first sit down and count the cost, whether he has enough to complete it? (Luke 14:28)

The application to birth control is that it seems wise for couples to realistically "count the cost" and see whether they have enough physical and emotional resources, and reasonable expectation of financial resources as well, to raise more children.

---

16. John S. Feinberg and Paul D. Feinberg, *Ethics for a Brave New World*, 2nd ed. (Wheaton, IL: Crossway, 2010), 305.

However, it also must be said that many modern families with four, five, or even more children often find that the Lord gives them the strength and resources needed for raising their children well "in the discipline and instruction of the Lord" (Eph. 6:4).

The broader consideration here is that all of life consists in deciding not to do some good things in order to be able to do some other good things. There are many more good things in the world to do than we can possibly achieve even in many lifetimes.

Later in this book I will consider the arguments for an alternative perspective, namely, that birth control is always wrong for Christian couples (see pp. 25–34).

D. MORALLY ACCEPTABLE AND MORALLY UNACCEPTABLE METHODS OF BIRTH CONTROL

Various methods of birth control prevent the husband's sperm from fertilizing the wife's ovum (egg), and thus they do not destroy any new human life. Therefore, they are *morally acceptable* means of birth control. According to the Life Issues Institute, this would include the use of a condom, a diaphragm, a sponge, a spermicide, and most birth-control pills.[17] The older "rhythm" method, now superseded by natural family planning (NFP), also falls in this category.[18] In

---

17. "Abortifacients: An Overview," Life Issues Institute, Inc., Sept. 29, 2014, http://www.lifeissues.org/2014/09/abortifacients-overview/.

18. Information on natural family planning can be found at National Family Planning International, http://nfpandmore.org/; the U.S. Department of Health and

addition, if a couple has reached a decision not to have any more children for their lifetimes, a vasectomy (for the man) or a tubal ligation (for the woman, commonly called having one's "tubes tied") would also be morally acceptable.

On the other hand, some methods of birth control allow conception to occur and then cause the death of the newly conceived child. As I have argued elsewhere with respect to abortion,[19] Scripture indicates that we should consider the unborn child to be a human person from the moment of conception (Ps. 51:5; see further discussion below, pp. 42–43). This is also evident from the fact that when the husband's sperm fertilizes the wife's ovum (egg), a new living creature with its own distinct DNA begins to form as cells divide and multiply. Birth-control methods that would cause the death of this newly conceived child (methods known as abortifacients) include the morning-after pills (RU-486 and ellaOne).[20]

The intrauterine device (IUD) should also be considered an abortifacient. This medical device allows a woman's egg to be fertilized by a man's sperm, but prevents the resulting embryo from being implanted in the mother's womb. According to Donna Harrison, a board-certified obstetrician-gynecologist, preventing an embryo from implanting

Human Services, https://www.hhs.gov/opa/pregnancy-prevention/non-hormonal -methods/natural-family-planning/index.html; and WebMd, http://www.webmd .com/sex/birth-control/features/today-natural-family-planning#1. The Roman Catholic Church, in particular, has a number of resources on natural family planning.

19. See Grudem, *Christian Ethics*, 566–72.

20. "Abortifacients: An Overview"; see also James Trussell, Elizabeth G. Raymond, and Kelly Cleland, "Emergency Contraception: A Last Chance to Prevent Unintended Pregnancy," Princeton University, Office of Population Research, November 2016, http://ec.princeton.edu/questions/ec-review.pdf.

effectively kills the embryo, and thus is an abortion.[21] Therefore, such a means of birth control is not morally acceptable on biblical grounds. (See also the discussion of modern reproductive technology below, pp. 37–69.)

E. HUSBANDS SHOULD BE CAREFUL NOT TO DENY TO THEIR WIVES FOR TOO LONG THE PRIVILEGE AND JOY OF HAVING CHILDREN

While I believe that using birth control for a limited time is morally permissible for couples, it is also important for husbands to realize that their wives frequently will have a deep, intense longing to bear children that their husbands may not be aware of. It was not Jacob who said to Rachel, but Rachel who said to Jacob in despair of her infertility, "Give me children, or I shall die!" (Gen. 30:1).

One example of the insensitivity husbands can show toward their wives in this area is the reaction of Elkanah to the sorrow felt by his wife Hannah when she had no children:

> And Elkanah, her husband, said to her, "Hannah, why do you weep? And why do you not eat? And why is your heart sad? *Am I not more to you than ten sons?*" (1 Sam. 1:8)

But Hannah felt this sorrow deeply, for "she was deeply distressed and prayed to the LORD and wept bitterly" (1 Sam. 1:10).

---

21. Donna Harrison, "Contraception That Kills," *National Review*, July 8, 2014, http://www.nationalreview.com/article/382172/contraception-kills-donna -harrison.

Psalm 113 emphasizes the joy that comes to a previously barren woman when God enables her to bear children:

> He gives the barren woman a home,
>> *making her the joyous mother of children.*
> Praise the Lord! (Ps. 113:9; see also Isa. 54:1)

By contrast, when Abram (later Abraham) was distressed over his childlessness, his focus was not on his personal longing to bear and raise a child, but on his lack of an heir:

> And Abram said, "Behold, you have given me no offspring, *and a member of my household will be my heir*." (Gen. 15:3)

F. AN ALTERNATIVE VIEWPOINT: ALL BIRTH CONTROL IS WRONG (OR ALL "ARTIFICIAL" BIRTH CONTROL IS WRONG)

In recent decades a "natural family planning" movement has gained influence among evangelical Christians. Such Christians oppose birth control (or most methods of birth control). They support their view with at least the following three arguments:

1. Children are a blessing; therefore, we should have many children.
2. We should trust God to decide how many children we should have.
3. Birth control is unnatural.

I will respond to these three arguments in the following sections.

1. Children Are a Blessing; Therefore, We Should Have Many Children. Mary Pride is an influential evangelical opponent of birth control. She makes the following argument:

> The two methods Christians use to plan their families—
> (1) spacing and (2) limiting family size—both have one thing in common: *they make a cut off point on how many blessings a family is willing to accept.* Can anyone find one single Bible verse that says Christians should refuse God's blessings? Children are an *unqualified* blessing, according to the Bible.[22]

My response to this argument is that it is based on reasoning that is mistaken and unbiblical. The reasoning, at its base, is this: if something is good or a blessing, we should seek to maximize it.

The problem with this reasoning is that there are many good things in life, many blessings from God, and we cannot possibly maximize all of them. Sleep is a good thing (Ps. 127:2), but God does not require us to get as much sleep as we possibly can (see the warning against sleeping too much in Prov. 6:10–11). Food is a good thing and a blessing from God, but it would be wrong to eat all that we can possibly eat. Work is also a blessing from God (Eccles. 2:24; 3:13; 5:18), but that does not mean we are required to work as

---

22. Mary Pride, *The Way Home: Beyond Feminism, Back to Reality* (Westchester, IL: Crossway, 1985), 76, emphasis in original.

much as we possibly can. The same could be said of physical exercise, giving to the poor, evangelism, worship, or Bible study.

Instead of the false principle "If something is good, you should seek to maximize it," God requires us to pray and exercise mature wisdom in seeking to know how to allocate the limited time we have among the various good activities available to us in this life.

Such mistaken reasoning as Pride offers is not limited to opponents of birth control. Often in Christian circles one hears exhortations of the type: "Since activity XYZ is good, you should do more of activity XYZ," where activity XYZ is teaching children in Sunday school, ministering to the poor, taking part in evangelistic campaigns—or having more children. But this exhortation fails to take into account God's individual callings on different people. God may be calling a person to focus more on activity ABC or activity DEF instead of activity XYZ.

Paul's direction is better:

> Only let each person lead *the life that the Lord has assigned to him*, and to which God has called him. This is my rule in all the churches. (1 Cor. 7:17)

"The life that the Lord has assigned" to each person is best determined by prayerful, wise consideration of one's own gifts and callings from God, and that might not include a calling for a married couple to raise as many children as they can physically conceive. Allowing people to have freedom to follow their own individual callings from God means that people will make many different decisions about which good activities to emphasize. Some will have many children, while others will have fewer children and will devote more time to different ministries and other worthwhile activities. Allowing for such freedom respects the diversity of callings within the church. "There are many parts, yet one body" (1 Cor. 12:20).

2. We Should Trust God to Decide How Many Children We Should Have. Pride also makes this argument:

> There *is* an alternative to scheming and plotting how many babies to have and when to have them. It can be summed up in three little words: trust and obey. If God is willing to plan my family for me . . . then why should I muddle up his plan with my ideas?[23]

This argument against birth control fails to recognize that God's sovereignty does not normally override the ordinary functioning of the natural world that he has created. We do not say to a farmer, "Trust God's sovereignty regarding how many weeds will grow in your field." If he did nothing to overcome the weeds, they would soon overgrow his field.

To take another example, my neighbors have a grapefruit tree that produces delicious grapefruits every year—so many that they cheerfully give them to the neighbors.

---

23. Pride, *The Way Home*, 77.

But they don't allow the grapefruits that fall from the tree to remain there and disperse their seeds on the ground, so that many more grapefruit trees eventually sprout! An advocate of "natural grapefruit tree planning" might tell them to "trust God to decide how many grapefruit trees you will have," but the result would be that they would soon have more grapefruit trees than they could ever care for. It is far wiser for them to exercise some grapefruit "birth control" and gather up the grapefruits that fall to the ground.

The important concept to remember here is that *God does not usually, in his sovereignty, override the natural, ordinary consequences of human actions.* If a couple decides that they will have sex often and "trust God" to decide how many children they will have, the answer is that God has already decided (through the way he has ordered the natural world and our physical bodies) that they will have many children (assuming the couple is in good reproductive health). To say they are *trusting God* for how many children they will have is something like throwing wildflower seeds on their backyard once a week for a year and then saying, "We are trusting God to decide how many flowers will grow in our backyard." If seeds are repeatedly tossed on fertile ground, flowers will bloom.

The broader principle is that God wants us to trust him *regarding his commands and his promises that he has given to us in Scripture.* But there is nothing in Scripture that tells us to avoid using birth control and then to trust him for how many children we will have. We are not authorized to trust him for things he has not promised or commanded.

Daniel Doriani wisely analyzes the appeal to trusting in God's sovereignty that is made by Christians who oppose birth control:

> The "no birth control" movement says family planning usurps God's sovereignty by banning children who might have existed. This misunderstands the way God works with human agents and other "secondary means," such as the weather. If I say family planning interferes with God's sovereignty, I might as well argue that I should not plan my vacation or my next meal or where I live lest I interfere with God's plan. This concept of God's sovereignty could justify every kind of laziness and inaction, including refusal of medical care. It also assumes what is to be proved, that God wants the couple to have more children and wants them to cooperate through "unprotected" intercourse. But perhaps God has not planned more children for the couple and wants them to cooperate by using birth control! Ignorance of God's will never excuses us from the honest work of discerning and planning.[24]

3. Birth Control Is Unnatural. This argument is often the unstated assumption behind many objections to birth

---

24. Daniel Doriani, "Birth Dearth or Bring on the Babies? Biblical Perspectives on Family-Planning," *Journal of Biblical Counseling* 12, no. 1 (Fall 1993): 33. The entire article (24–35) contains many helpful insights regarding Christian arguments about birth control.

control: since sex without birth control is "natural," and since this "natural" process often leads to more babies, having more babies is morally right (or is God's will for us).

In response to this argument, we must reply that God does not command us simply to follow what is "natural," but rather to follow his commands in Scripture. (Here we differ with the Roman Catholic view that places much greater emphasis on what they perceive as "natural law.")

The Bible often directs us on a course that differs from the course of nature. With respect to sexual intercourse itself, God does not command us to do what is "natural"; rather, he commands us to limit sex to a married relationship rather than following our "natural instincts," which would sometimes lead us to have sex with a number of different people.

It is important to keep in mind that God changed the order of the natural world at the time of the fall, and this means that our highest ideal is not simply to let "untouched nature" take its course. After Adam and Eve sinned, God said, "Cursed is the ground because of you; in pain you shall eat of it all of the days of your life; thorns and thistles it shall bring forth for you" (Gen. 3:17–18). Suddenly, life in the natural world became more difficult and painful.

When we couple this alteration that God imposed on the natural world with God's command to "subdue" the earth (Gen. 1:28), it is right to conclude that we should often take active steps to change or even overcome the course of untouched nature. This applies not only to the plants of the field, but also to our physical bodies, for which we often need medicines to remedy some disability or illness.

We modify nature in many ways. We prune fruit trees; we thin carrots; we clear out trees in order to plant crops; we kill weeds; and we put up barriers to exclude wild animals. In all of these ways we are interfering with the course of nature in order to more effectively obey God.

This is especially relevant to the question of childbirth, because after Adam and Eve sinned, God changed the effects that childbirth would have on a woman's body:

To the woman he said,

> "*I will surely multiply your pain in* childbearing;
> in pain you shall bring forth children."
> (Gen. 3:16)

This indicates that childbirth is much more painful and probably much more taxing on a woman's body than it would have been prior to the fall.

So if Adam and Eve had not sinned, and if there had been no curse placed upon the woman with regard to childbearing, it is possible that Eve, in her unfallen body, could have easily borne 15, 20, or more children, at a rate of one per year, while feeling no pain and suffering, and experiencing no lasting wear and tear on her body. But this was no longer the case after the curse was imposed. What is now "natural" will not always be what is best.

In addition, it is possible that Genesis 3:16 also indicates an increase in the frequency of a woman's fertility, more than her body is suited to bear in her fallen state. The King James Version (and the New King James Version) provides an alternative translation:

I will greatly multiply thy sorrow *and thy conception.* (KJV)

I will greatly multiply your sorrow *and your conception.* (NKJV)

This translation is a grammatically legitimate and entirely literal translation of the Hebrew term *wehēronēk*, "and your conception." Based on this translation, it is possible that, prior to the fall, Eve's period of fertility would have occurred less frequently, perhaps once every year or two years. And this would have meant that sexual intercourse for almost the entire year would not have been for the purpose of procreation, but for the purpose of mutual enjoyment and companionship.[25]

Related to the idea that we should follow what is "natural" is the idea that procreation is the main purpose (or perhaps even the only legitimate purpose) for sexual

---

25. However, in defense of most other translations, including the ESV, the vast majority of translation committees have understood the Hebrew expression to be an example of *hendiadys*, the use of two words joined by "and" to express a single idea, in this case not just "pain and childbearing" but "pain in childbearing," a single idea. This is also a grammatically legitimate translation, and translation committees have tended to favor it, probably because of a conviction that the overwhelming prochild perspective of Scripture would not easily be compatible with the idea that increased fertility was a part of the curse.

Yet I do not want to dismiss the possibility of the KJV translation too quickly. One veteran missionary who had worked with women in poor countries for several decades told me, for example, that she had frequently seen the devastating physical effects on poor women of 15 or 20 sequential years of childbirth.

intercourse. But surely that idea is not found in Scripture. Sexual intercourse also gives realization to the "one flesh" union that is the essence of marriage (see Gen. 2:24; Eph. 5:31). And sexual intimacy in marriage is also given by God for the purpose of mutual pleasure and deep companionship (see Prov. 5:18–19; Song of Solomon). Because procreation is not the only purpose for sexual intercourse, sex within marriage is also a good thing during a woman's nonfertile times each month, as well as after she experiences menopause.

As for the claim that procreation is the primary purpose of sexual intercourse, it is difficult to know how any criteria could be found that would prove this. If God creates something with multiple purposes, who are we to determine that one purpose is primary and others are secondary?

In conclusion, these three arguments against birth control are not persuasive.

G. HOW CAN A COUPLE KNOW HOW MANY CHILDREN TO HAVE?

If children are a blessing, and if it is good to have children, and if birth control is acceptable for at least some periods of time in a marriage, then how can a couple decide how many children they should have?

Scripture does not give us one answer that fits every married couple. In such a case, we should be gracious and allow people to have a wide variety of different answers because of their different individual callings from God.

In general, couples should pray for God's wisdom, which may become increasingly clear to them over several months or years:

> *If any of you lacks wisdom, let him ask God*, who gives generously to all without reproach, and it will be given him. But let him ask in faith, with no doubting, for the one who doubts is like a wave of the sea that is driven and tossed by the wind. (James 1:5–6)

If they are comfortable doing so, couples might also decide to seek the counsel of others, through whom God will often give us wisdom.

The conclusions I have argued for in this section imply that a couple's fundamental perspective in this decision should be that children are a blessing from the Lord, and that having children is a good thing and pleasing to God (Gen. 1:28; Ps. 127:3–5; 128:3–4; Mal. 2:15; 1 Tim. 5:14). But it is also right for them to "count the cost" (Luke 14:28) of undertaking such a weighty responsibility. If they deeply desire to have more children, then it is likely that God is calling them to do this, and they should willingly trust him to provide for their needs and enable them to provide for their family (1 Tim. 5:8), so long as they are not making a reckless, foolish decision that is in essence demanding miraculous provision from God. But if one or both of them is strongly opposed to having more children, and if that opposition is based on biblical, godly desires, then that opposition should be weighed heavily in the decision-making process, and use of birth control would seem appropriate.

In between those two situations, a couple may feel unsure or ambivalent about having more children, and in that case they will probably decide not to actively try to prevent pregnancy, to thank God that he often grants us the blessing of children, and then to wait and see if God in his sovereignty will provide them with more children.

However, there are two errors that should clearly be avoided: (1) basing a decision on fear, selfishness, and the unsanctified expectations of a non-Christian culture, and thus failing to obey God's calling; and (2) basing a decision on a reckless, irresponsible sort of "faith" that is not from God but is only a projection of a person's wrongful motives.

The kind of attitude Christians have toward others who have few or many children is also important. In this regard, as with getting married or not getting married, "each has his own gift from God, one of one kind and one of another" (1 Cor. 7:7), and Christians should respect and honor the different decisions that other families have made in this regard: "Who are you to pass judgment on the servant of another? It is before his own master that he stands or falls" (Rom. 14:4; see also v. 10).

PART 2: INFERTILITY AND REPRODUCTIVE TECHNOLOGY

Infertility is the inability of a couple to conceive and bear children due to a lack of normal function in either the man's or the woman's reproductive system. Modern medical developments provide several solutions for infertility, and this section will provide guidelines for evaluating them. At the end of this section, I will also consider a related issue, adoption.

A. INFERTILITY

1. Infertility in the Old and New Testaments. Infertility has been a source of deep sorrow for both men and women, but especially for women, for all of human history, as we see from some of the early chapters of the Bible. Sarah (Sarai) was unable to bear children to Abraham (Gen. 11:30; 16:1) for most of her life, until she miraculously bore Isaac in her old age (see 21:1–7). Jacob's wife Rachel was unable to bear children for a long time after her marriage to Jacob (29:31), as was Samson's mother, the wife of Manoah (Judg. 13:2). Hannah, the mother of Samuel, cried out to the Lord in deep sorrow because of her infertility (1 Sam. 1:2–18). In the New Testament, Zechariah and Elizabeth "had no child, because Elizabeth was barren, and both were advanced in years" (Luke 1:7), but, again through God's miraculous intervention, Elizabeth eventually gave birth to John the Baptist (vv. 57–66). These narrative examples show that *overcoming infertility is something that pleases God*, and is often a manifestation of his special blessing on a couple.

In addition, there are some general passages that show God's great blessing when "he gives the barren woman a home, making her the joyous mother of children. Praise the LORD!" (Ps. 113:9; see also Ex. 23:26; Deut. 7:14; Isa. 54:1; Gal. 4:27). These passages are entirely consistent with the perspective that I presented in the previous section, that the broad teaching of the Bible is that children are a great blessing from God: "Behold, children are a heritage from the LORD, the fruit of the womb a reward" (Ps. 127:3; see also Gen. 1:28; Ps. 128:3–4; Mal. 2:15; 1 Tim. 5:14; see also pp. 12–17 above).

Because of the consistent force of these biblical passages, it is right to consider infertility as something that we should seek to overcome with the confidence that God is pleased with such efforts. Infertility should not be something about which we are indifferent, such as the color of our hair or eyes, but rather something we see as another result of the fall, one of the diseases and disabilities that entered the human race after Adam and Eve sinned. Infertility was not part of God's good creation as he originally made it or intended it to function.

2. A Feeling of Grief in Childlessness. God in his wisdom shows compassion and awareness of the deep grief of childlessness in several passages, such as the stories of Rachel (Gen. 30:1) and Hannah (1 Sam. 1:5–10).

The deep grief that is felt by childless couples must not be minimized or dismissed lightly by others, especially pastors and counselors, but also friends. Because only women are able to bear and nurse children, this grief can be especially acute for wives due to a sense of loss at not being able to have a jointly conceived child, at not having the experience of pregnancy, at not going through the birth and breastfeeding of a child, and at not being able to serve as a mother for her own children.

3. Faith in the Midst of Sorrow. Sometimes a childless couple will wonder if their situation is a result of God's displeasure or discipline, and this will make it difficult for them to believe that God has good purposes for them and for their lives. But the example of Zechariah and Elizabeth in the beginning of Luke's Gospel shows that infertility can happen even to a godly, morally exemplary couple, because Zechariah and Elizabeth "were both righteous before God" (Luke 1:6; this is a reminder that their infertility was not a result of their individual sin), yet they were still unable to have children:

> In the days of Herod, king of Judea, there was a priest named Zechariah, of the division of Abijah. And he had a wife from the daughters of Aaron, and her name was Elizabeth. *And they were both righteous before God, walking blamelessly in all the commandments and statutes of the Lord. But they had no child,* because

Elizabeth was barren, and both were advanced in years. (Luke 1:5–7)

It is important to recognize that the inability to have children is a difficult trial, a kind of suffering that many couples endure privately and silently. In such situations, Scripture passages that deal with trials and suffering in the Christian life are often helpful in encouraging people's faith:

> In this [your salvation] you rejoice, though now for a little while, if necessary, *you have been grieved by various trials*, so that the tested genuineness of your faith—more precious than gold that perishes though it is tested by fire—may be found to result in praise and glory and honor at the revelation of Jesus Christ. Though you have not seen him, you love him. Though you do not now see him, you believe in him and rejoice with joy that is inexpressible and filled with glory, obtaining the outcome of your faith, the salvation of your souls. (1 Pet. 1:6–9; see also James 1:2–4)

Here Peter encourages believers going through trials to continue in faith, which is very precious to God, and which will result in great reward. In addition, he encourages suffering believers to love Christ and believe in him, for that relationship with him will fill them with joy.

It will also be an encouragement for infertile couples to recall that neither Jesus nor Paul had physical children, but both found great fulfillment in the ministries that God had entrusted to them. They had many spiritual children, who came into the kingdom of God and were nurtured by their ministries.

As I mentioned in the previous section, the New Testament several times puts a positive emphasis on spiritual children who are the result of a person's ministry. Paul tells the Corinthian church, "I became your father in Christ Jesus through the gospel" (1 Cor. 4:15). He calls the Galatian Christians "my little children" (Gal. 4:19). He calls Timothy "my true child in the faith" (1 Tim. 1:2) and similarly calls Titus "my true child in a common faith" (Titus 1:4). And Peter refers to Mark, who often traveled with him, as "Mark, my son" (1 Pet. 5:13).

B. THREE MORAL PRINCIPLES TO CONSIDER IN RELATION TO REPRODUCTIVE TECHNOLOGY

1. Modern Medicine in General Is Morally Good. Modern medicine can be used to overcome many diseases and disabilities today. We should view this as a good thing, and as something for which we can give thanks to God.

God put resources in the earth for us to discover and develop, including resources that are useful for medicinal purposes, and he gave us the wisdom and the desire to do this. The warrant for this is found in God's command to Adam and Eve to "subdue" the earth (Gen. 1:28), and it is reinforced by the fact that all of the medicines we have today are made from resources found in the earth, and "*the earth is the* LORD's and the fullness thereof, the world and those who dwell therein" (Ps. 24:1).

Jesus's ministry of healing also indicated that God is pleased when we try to help people overcome diseases and disabilities:

> Now when the sun was setting, all those who had any who were sick with various diseases brought them to him, and *he laid his hands on every one of them and healed them*. (Luke 4:40)

This was a common pattern in Jesus's earthly ministry, and the inclusive nature of the expression "*all* those who had *any* who were sick with *various* diseases" allows us to suppose that Jesus also healed the infertility of many women (and men) who had previously been unable to conceive and bear children.

Therefore, it seems morally right to support and welcome advances in medicine that today can bring health to people with various diseases and disabilities, including infertility.

2. We Should Treat the Unborn Child as a Human Person from the Moment of Conception. As I have argued extensively elsewhere,[26] various passages in Scripture lead us to consider the unborn child as a human person from the moment of conception. In thinking back on the beginning of his existence as a sinner, David mentioned his sinful-

---

26 Grudem, *Christian Ethics*, 566–86 (chap. 21).

ness even at the moment of his conception: "I was brought forth in iniquity, and *in sin did my mother conceive me*" (Ps. 51:5). In addition, David said to God, "You knitted me together in my mother's womb" (139:13). In the old covenant, if an unborn child died, even because of an accidental injury, the one who caused the unborn child to die was subject to capital punishment (see Ex. 21:22–25: "You shall pay life for life"). Jacob and Esau were viewed as two unique children who would become two nations struggling within Rebekah's womb (Gen. 25:22–23). And Elizabeth, in the sixth month of her pregnancy, said, "The baby in my womb leaped for joy"—surely a human action (Luke 1:44).

These passages are relevant for the question of reproductive technologies, because they mean that we should not condone any such technology that will certainly lead to the death of even one unborn child who was conceived when the man's sperm fertilized the woman's egg, the cells began to divide, and the human embryo began to grow into a little baby.

3. God Intends That a Child Should Be Conceived by and Born to a Man and Woman Who Are Married to Each Other. I affirm this third principle with somewhat more hesitation than the first two because this principle is not derived from any direct command of Scripture, but rather from a pattern of biblical narratives and probable implications from biblical moral commands about some related topics.

Many contemporary ethical questions related to reproductive technology have to do with the medical possibility of a woman becoming pregnant and bearing a child *even when the child's biological father is not that woman's husband*. But the entire scope of the biblical narratives and biblical moral standards views this situation as contrary to God's intended plan for the birth of a child.[27]

At the beginning of creation God said to Adam and Eve (who were husband and wife), "Be fruitful and multiply and fill the earth" (Gen. 1:28). This verse by itself does not say that no other means of producing children would be pleasing to God, but it is the foundational pattern for marriage in the entire Bible, and it is the first instance of the command to be fruitful. (Scripture calls Adam and Eve "the man and his wife" in Gen. 2:25, and uses the relationship between Adam and Eve as the pattern for marriage generally in v. 24.)

God's repeated commands against adultery (Ex. 20:14; Lev. 20:10; Deut. 5:18; Prov. 6:32; Matt. 15:19; Rom. 13:9; James 2:11; 2 Pet. 2:14) also support this idea. One reason that sexual intercourse should occur only within the context of marriage is that this guarantees that children will only be born to a man and a woman who are married to each other.

Another piece of evidence supporting this conclusion is found in the detailed laws in Exodus:

---

27. The situation of the virgin birth of Jesus to his mother, Mary, is an event that was unique in the entire history of the human race because, in the wise providence of God, Jesus had no biological human father.

> If a man seduces a virgin who is not betrothed and lies
> with her, he shall give the bride-price for her and make
> her his wife. (Ex. 22:16; the rare exception is seen in
> v. 17, but the general principle is that marriage should
> occur; see also Deut. 22:28–29)

Here again, the specific provision of the law guaranteed
that if a man and a woman had sexual intercourse, they
would have to get married, once again guaranteeing that a
child would be born in the context of a man and a woman
who are married to each other.

Jesus's teachings against divorce gave further protection
that guaranteed that children would be born within marriage.
The general principle is, "What therefore God has joined
together, let not man separate" (Matt. 19:6). The only exceptions (where divorce is allowed) are cases in which the marriage has been so seriously defiled by adultery or by long-term
desertion that the spouses cannot be reconciled, but those are
intended to be rare situations, and in such cases the conception
of further children would not ordinarily occur in any case.

The prohibitions against "sexual immorality" (in older
translations "fornication," Greek, *porneia*) also seek to en-
sure that sexual intercourse occurs only within the context of
marriage. This would guarantee that children would be conceived only within the context of marriage (see 1 Cor. 6:18;
2 Cor. 12:21; Gal. 5:19; Eph. 5:3; Col. 3:5; 1 Thess. 4:3).

Finally, there is no indication anywhere in Scripture
that God ever considered it morally right for a child to be

conceived by a man and a woman who were not married to each other.

This broad pattern of scriptural teaching, then, leads me to conclude that a child should be conceived by and born to a man and a woman who are married to each other, and in no other situation or relationship.

C. SOME MODERN REPRODUCTIVE TECHNOLOGIES ARE MORALLY ACCEPTABLE

The general category for various medical methods to help people have children is "assisted reproductive technology" (abbreviated ART). In this section I will consider some specific kinds of modern assisted reproductive technology in light of the three moral principles above. However, a word of caution is in order. Medical technology in this area is developing at a remarkable speed, and it is impossible to predict what new procedures might be available in the next several years. Other evangelical ethicists have analyzed reproductive technologies in more detail than I am able to do in this section,[28] and I hope that they and others like them will continue such detailed studies.

However, I also hope that the individual topics that I discuss in this section will provide a pattern of ethical

---

28. In the bibliography at the end of this book, see especially the works by John S. Feinberg and Paul D. Feinberg, John M. Frame, John F. Kilner, C. Ben Mitchell, Scott B. Rae, and David VanDrunen. The website of the Center for Bioethics and Human Dignity at Trinity International University also has extensive resources on many detailed questions in bioethics: https://cbhd.org/. I also recommend the bioethics statement on this subject produced by the Christian Medical and Dental Associations; see https://cmda.org/wp-content/uploads/2018/04/Assisted ReproductiveTechnology-2010.pdf.

reasoning that readers will find useful in evaluating future techniques and procedures.

The three conclusions from the previous section may be summarized as follows:

1. Modern medicine in general is morally good.
2. We should treat the unborn child as a human person from the moment of conception.
3. God intends that a child should be conceived by and born to a man and woman who are married to each other.

These three principles give us a useful perspective from which we can conclude that some kinds of modern reproductive technology are morally acceptable and other kinds are not.

1. Artificial Insemination by Husband (AIH). The process of artificial insemination by husband does not violate any of the biblical principles named above. It simply enables a wife to become pregnant by her husband's sperm when, for some reason, it is physically unlikely or impossible for this to happen through ordinary sexual intercourse. The husband's sperm is first collected and then injected into the wife's cervix or uterus using a needleless syringe or other medical device. The child is conceived by and born to a man and a woman who are married to each other. No unborn human person (or embryo) is destroyed in the process. And the wonderful result is that infertility is overcome for this couple.

2. In Vitro Fertilization without Destruction of Embryos. In vitro fertilization (abbreviated IVF) is the process of joining together a woman's egg (ovum) and a husband's sperm in a laboratory rather than inside a woman's body. (The Latin phrase *in vitro* means "in glass.")

Evangelical Christians differ on the moral acceptability of this procedure, as I will indicate below (some respected evangelical writers argue that in vitro fertilization is always morally unacceptable). My own position is that, in principle, there should be no moral objection to in vitro fertilization according to scriptural standards, as long as no human embryos are destroyed in the process, because it is once again simply enabling an infertile husband and wife to have children and thereby overcoming their infertility by means of modern medicine.

Someone might object that this is not the "natural" process of conception through sexual intercourse that God intended, but such an argument must assume a definition of "natural" that arbitrarily excludes modern medical means from what we consider part of nature. Is not the laboratory equipment that is used for in vitro fertilization also made from resources that God planted in the earth? Are not the medical researchers and medical technicians, with all their wisdom and skill, part of God's creation also?

To cite another analogy, consider a woman who uses a modern thermometer to take her body temperature every day in order to find out the best time to have intercourse so that she will be able to conceive a child. Is this an "unnatural" process because she uses a modern medical thermometer in order to know when she is ovulating? Surely not. The thermometer is made from part of the natural world that God created. Similarly, consider a husband who uses Viagra or a similar modern medicine to overcome erectile dysfunction so that he and his wife can have intercourse and conceive a baby. Is that process to be rejected as "unnatural" because he is using modern medicine to overcome his medical problem? Surely not. The Viagra is made from materials that God placed in the natural world, and so it is also part of nature considered in a broad sense.

Therefore, there seems to be no valid reason to reject in vitro fertilization on the ground that it is not part of the natural process that God established for the conception of children. The essential considerations in this issue are all satisfied: modern medicine is used to overcome a disability, no unborn children's lives are destroyed, and the child is conceived by and born to a man and a woman who are married to each other.

However, in vitro fertilization is often carried out in a way that destroys multiple human embryos, and therefore wrongly results in the destruction of human life. This happens because, in order to increase the probability of pregnancy, more of the wife's eggs may be fertilized in laboratory equipment than are actually implanted in her womb.

In most cases, couples going through in vitro fertilization where multiple embryos are created can indicate one of the following options for the handling of any remaining embryos:

1. Freezing (cryopreservation) of unimplanted embryos for use by the couple in any future treatment cycles.
2. Anonymously donating the embryos for use by other infertile couples. (See the section on "Embryo Adoption" below.)
3. Allowing the embryos to develop in the laboratory until they perish, at which time they are discarded, which is usually within six to eight days of collection.[29]

The fertilization of multiple eggs is not necessary, however. Technological development of in vitro fertilization has reached the point where, if the couple wishes to fertilize only one egg or two and then have them both implanted in the mother's womb, that can be done. In fact, one 2012 British study found that women should never have more than two eggs implanted. "Previous research—before more modern techniques for IVF—still showed that implanting three [embryos] increased the likelihood of successful live birth rate, compared with the transfer of two or one," said the lead researcher, Debbie Lawlor of the University of Bristol. "Our research shows this is no longer the case."[30] In such cases, where no embryos are destroyed, I think that in vitro fertilization is morally acceptable.

---

29. See "In Vitro Fertilization (IVF)," The Mayo Clinic, http://www.mayoclinic.org/tests-procedures/in-vitro-fertilization/details/how-you-prepare/ppc-20206941.
30. Cited in Catharine Pearson, "IVF Study Shows Two Eggs are Good, 3 Too Many," *Huffington Post*, Jan. 18, 2012, http://www.huffingtonpost.com/2012/01/12/ivf-study-shows-2-eggs-ar_n_1202020.html.

John Feinberg and Paul Feinberg disagree with my position here and argue that IVF is morally unacceptable, even when only one egg is fertilized, because the success rate is so low in such cases. They write:

> We believe the embryo is human and a person from conception onward. . . . Our views on the embryo's status lead to our greatest moral objection to IVF, namely, its waste and loss of embryonic life. . . . If the success rate of IVF had risen to 95 percent or even 80–85 percent, we would be more sympathetic to it, but . . . IVF technology is currently nowhere near such success rates. We find the loss of so much human life morally unacceptable. . . . Success rates [are] at best only about 17 percent when one embryo is used. . . . Too many human lives are lost to think this is morally acceptable.[31]

I have much respect for the Feinbergs' book, which I used as my primary textbook for teaching Christian ethics for many years. I agree with their conclusions far more often than I disagree. In addition, both John and Paul Feinberg were valued colleagues of mine when I taught at Trinity Evangelical Divinity School. I find their objection at this point to be significant and I take it seriously, but in the end I am not persuaded by it.

---

31. John S. Feinberg and Paul D. Feinberg, *Ethics for a Brave New World*, 2nd ed. (Wheaton, IL: Crossway, 2010), 424–25. British author John Ling also objects to IVF: see John R. Ling, *Bioethical Issues: Understanding and Responding to the Culture of Death*, revised and updated ed. (Leominster, UK: Day One Publications, 2014). He summarizes his objections here: http://www.johnling.co.uk/thirtyyears.htm.

My response is that fertilizing only one egg or two at a time, and implanting these with the hope that they will survive, is far different from the common practice of in vitro fertilization, where several eggs are fertilized and then most of them are intentionally destroyed. In that case, there is a willful destruction of human lives. But with the fertilization of only one or two eggs at a time, the intent of the doctor and the husband and wife is that all of the fertilized eggs will live and come to normal birth. Therefore, I still think that this kind of in vitro fertilization is morally acceptable.[32]

This does not mean that couples have an obligation to try in vitro fertilization, only that it is a morally acceptable thing to do. Many couples may reason that the process is too expensive for them to afford. On average, the cost of a basic IVF cycle in the United States ranges from about $12,000 to $15,000. Another less-complicated process called "Mini-IVF" is approximately $5,000 to $7,000.[33]

Others may reason that the likelihood of success for the procedure is so slim that they do not want to embark

---

32. Two other objections that may be brought against IVF are (1) that advances in IVF technology are often developed by researchers who intentionally destroy hundreds of embryos, and (2) that IVF separates conception from the "one-flesh" sexual union (Gen. 2:24) in which God intended it to occur. I recognize that some readers will find these objections persuasive, but I do not because (1) I do not think we are responsible to avoid using all modern technologies developed by sinful human beings at various times and places around the world, and (2) no command of Scripture says that the conception of a child by a husband and wife must only occur through such a "one-flesh" union. I want to be careful both to teach all the ethical standards that Scripture teaches and also not to prohibit what Scripture does not forbid.

33. "IVF Costs—In Vitro Fertilization Costs," Internet Health Resources, Infertility Resources, https://www.ihr.com/infertility/ivf/ivf-in-vitro-fertilization-cost.html.

on such a difficult process. According to the Society of Assisted Reproductive Technologies (SART) in 2017, the live birth rate per IVF cycle with their own eggs is 54.7 percent among women younger than 35; 40.6 percent for those aged 35 to 37; and 25.6 percent for those aged 38 to 40. The success rate drops to 12.8 percent in those older than 40, and success in women older than 44 is rare, approximately 4.4 percent.[34]

A Swedish study found that a woman who had just one embryo implanted in her womb had nearly as great a chance of getting pregnant as a woman who had two or more embryos implanted. Transferring only one embryo also reduced the chances of twins being born with low birth weight and the accompanying complications.[35]

Another consideration is that a couple may decide that embarking on another pregnancy carries increased risks for the mother's health that are too significant for them to think they should try IVF. In such cases also, the *medical possibility* and the *moral acceptability* of trying in vitro fertilization do not mean that there is any obligation on them to use this procedure if they do not want to do so.

3. Embryo Adoption. Often during the process of in vitro fertilization, more of a woman's eggs are fertilized in the

---

34. "Final Cumulative Outcome Per Egg Retrieval Cycle," Society of Assisted Reproductive Technologies, 2014, https://www.sartcorsonline.com/rptCSR_Public MultYear.aspx.

35. "Good Results with Only One Egg in In-Vitro Fertilization," *Science Daily*, Dec. 14, 2004, https://www.sciencedaily.com/releases/2004/12/041203 091047.htm.

laboratory than are implanted in her womb. As noted above, instead of destroying these embryos, some couples decide to freeze them, in case they decide to have more children later or for other reasons. As of 2015, it is estimated that there are more than one million frozen embryos in storage in the United States alone.[36] Many of them will never be claimed or used by the original parents. What should be done with these embryos?

One possibility is that other couples might adopt the embryos, have them implanted in the wife's womb, and allow them to grow and be born as normal children. Sometimes these children are called "snowflake children."[37]

While we should not encourage or give approval to the process of creating embryos that will not be used in the first place, once these embryos have been created, they seem to be in a situation very similar to that of orphans. They are very, very young children who have not yet been born and whose parents are no longer taking care of them.

In this case, the Bible's encouragement that we should care for orphans seems applicable:

---

36. John Burger, "Frozen Embryo Population in the U.S. Hits 1 Million," *Aleteia*, June 18, 2015, http://aleteia.org/2015/06/18/frozen-embryo-population-in-the-us-hits-1-million-mark/.

37. The term "snowflake children" refers to the children that result from the adoption of frozen embryos left over from in vitro fertilization. These embryos are transferred to infertile couples via *embryo adoption*. After adoption, the child has legal parents other than the man and woman whose sperm and egg originally conceived the embryo. The legal process of taking ownership of an embryo differs from that of traditional adoption. For more information, see https://www.nightlight.org/snowflakes-embryo-adoption-donation/embryo-adoption/.

Religion that is pure and undefiled before God the Father is this: *to visit orphans and widows in their affliction*, and to keep oneself unstained from the world. (James 1:27; see also Hos. 14:3)[38]

If we consider these frozen embryos as "orphans" who have been abandoned by their parents, then it clearly seems morally right for couples to adopt them, bring them to birth, and raise them in their own families as their own adopted children. In fact, God may bring much blessing to those who adopt and raise these embryos as children.[39]

Someone may wonder if there is damage to the physical or mental development of these children as a result of their existing in a frozen state over a period of time, sometimes for several years. But the surprising evidence shows that such snowflake children will often grow to be healthy and normal, and some are even now entering adulthood. For example, Hannah Strege, the first adopted frozen embryo, born on December 31, 1998, is not only perfectly healthy, but has traveled to Washington, DC, several times to testify before Congress as part of an effort to stop the killing of frozen embryos for stem cell research.[40] Another girl, Marley Jade,

---

38. Several Old Testament passages about "the fatherless" also show God's care for children who are unable to care for or protect themselves. See Ex. 22:22; Deut. 10:18; 24:17, 19–21; 26:12–13; 27:19; Pss. 10:14, 18; 68:5; 82:3; 146:9; Isa. 1:17; Jer. 7:6; 22:3; Zech. 7:10.

39. Feinberg and Feinberg also agree that adopting these frozen embryos and using them to produce babies is morally right; see *Ethics for a Brave New World*, 430–32.

40. Marilyn Synek, "A Person Is a Person No Matter How Small (Or Frozen)," *National Right to Life News Today*, Jan. 8, 2015, http://www.nationalrighttolifenews.org/news/2015/01/a-person-is-a-person-no-matter-how-small-or-frozen/.

born to a Denver couple on June 3, 2016, had been frozen for more than 17 years. Little Marley is perfectly healthy.[41]

Someone may object that adopting such an embryo and bringing it to birth as a normal child violates our earlier principle that God intends a child to be conceived by and born to a man and woman who are married to each other. But in these cases the child has already been conceived and already exists. Even if the child will not be born to the parents who *conceived it*, that child will be *born to a man and a woman who are married to each other*, and this is a far better result than being destroyed as an embryo.

But should a single or divorced woman be allowed by herself to adopt such a frozen embryo and bring him or her to birth and raise him or her as a child? This is a difficult question, and there is room for Christians to differ on the answer. While some might argue that this should not be permitted because being raised in a single-parent household is much more difficult for children, it seems to me that, from the child's perspective, it is still much better to grow up in a single-parent household than to die as a discarded embryo or to exist perpetually as a frozen embryo for decades to come. If the society decides through the political process that it is acceptable for single parents to adopt children once the children are born (and many societies have con-

41. Sara McGinnis, "Meet the Baby Girl Who Spent Over 17 Years as a Frozen Embryo," BabyCenter, Oct. 17, 2016, http://blogs.babycenter.com/mom_stories /embryo-adoption-10172016-infertility-snowflakes/.

cluded that it is right),[42] then there seems to be no reason to prohibit a single mother from adopting an unborn child and bringing him or her to birth.

4. Prefertilization Genetic Screening for Genetic Diseases. It is now possible to genetically screen a husband prior to fertilization of a woman's egg via in vitro fertilization or prior to artificial insemination by the husband. Such screening can determine if certain genetically determined diseases will be passed on from the father to the children. Since the male sperm by itself is not yet a human person, I see no moral objection to this procedure in itself, if used to prevent the conception of a child who would likely have a serious genetically transmitted disease (such screening can now test for cystic fibrosis, heart malformation, hemophilia, Huntington's disease, and sexually transmitted diseases such as syphilis, gonorrhea, and chlamydia).[43]

However, the same procedure could also be used not just to prevent diseases, but to allow the parents to choose among various types of perfectly healthy children. For

---

42. In the United States, single-parent adoption is legal in all 50 states. Some states have restrictions based on age, sexual orientation, criminal record, and state residency. See "Can Single Parents Adopt a Child?" Considering Adoption, https://consideringadoption.com/adopting/types-of-adoption/can-single-parents-adopt-a-child. It is estimated that 5 percent to 10 percent of all adoptions are done by singles. See "Single Parent Adoption," Adoption Services, http://www.adoptionservices.org/adoption_special/adoption_single.htm. Other countries that permit adoptions by single parents from other countries (with restrictions) are Haiti, Russia, China, Ethiopia, Guatemala, Vietnam, and Kazakhstan. See "Single Parent International Adoption," Single Parent Center, Dec. 16, 2016, http://www.singleparentcenter.net/single-parent-international-adoption/.

43. "New guidelines for screening of sperm, egg and embryo donors in the UK," British Fertility Society, Jan. 9, 2009, https://britishfertilitysociety.org.uk/press-release/new-guidelines-for-screening-of-sperm-egg-and-embryo-donors-in-the-uk/.

example, prior to fertilization, a couple might decide that they want to have a baby boy, and therefore only use sperm that contain a Y chromosome. Or they might decide that they want to have a baby girl, and therefore decide to use sperm that contain no Y chromosome. Future types of selection might include the possibility of choosing the minimum height to which a child will grow, color of eyes or hair, or even IQ level. Would this be right?

While such genetic screening processes do not involve new human life being put to death (because fertilization has not occurred), I would seriously question the motives of couples who would seek to make such selections. These are not cases of attempting to prevent diseases that are a result of the fall and of sin and death coming into the world, but rather are choices among the wonderful diversity and variety of human persons that would have resulted from God's creation at the beginning, even with no sin or death in the world. Especially regarding the matter of sex selection, does the preference for a boy or a girl reflect some underlying prejudice that girls are better than boys or boys are better than girls? This would be contrary to God's creation of both men and women as wonderful bearers of his image.[44]

---

44. See Paige Comstock Cunningham, "Baby-Making: The Fractured Fulfillment of Huxley's *Brave New World*, Part II," *Dignitas* 18, no. 2 (2011): 1, 6–9, https://cbhd.org/content/baby-making-pt-2the-fractured-fulfillment-huxleys-brave-new-world. Cunningham sees parallels between the eugenics movement of the early 20th century and the recent increase in genetic screening for sex selection or other characteristics as parents seek to have "perfect" babies.

D. OTHER MODERN REPRODUCTIVE TECHNOLOGIES ARE MORALLY UNACCEPTABLE

The same three moral principles listed above lead us to conclude that other reproductive technologies are morally unacceptable.

1. In Vitro Fertilization with Selective Reduction. In many uses of in vitro fertilization, numerous eggs are fertilized, then the doctor chooses the one or possibly two embryos that look most likely to survive. The doctor implants those embryos in the woman's womb and then destroys the others. But this is the destruction of human life, and should not be considered morally acceptable.

This process is often accompanied by preimplantation genetic diagnosis (PGD).[45] This is the most commonly used genetic screening for disease in the embryo, and is done around five to seven days after fertilization. One cell (or sometimes two) is removed from the embryo "conceived" by in vitro fertilization prior to implanting the embryo into the mother. Since this cell is like all others in the child's body, it contains the entire genetic complement of that individual, a combination of both the mother's and father's genomes (one of each gene from each parent).

Just as any living person (child or adult) can be genetically tested using a cell from that person (typically done through

45. I am grateful to Dr. Jacque Chadwick for her initial draft of these two paragraphs, and for helpful counsel at several other points in this entire book.

a swab from the mouth, collecting saliva that contains cells), so this cell from the embryo can be tested prior to the embryo's implantation in the mother's womb (thus the name of the procedure). Therefore, a decision can be made whether or not to implant the embryo based on its genetic makeup.

In addition, this procedure can easily be adapted to promote a form of eugenics, the belief that only those who are "desirable" should be allowed to live. Similarities to the theories of the American eugenics movement of the early twentieth century cause serious concern.

Similar to in vitro fertilization with selective reduction is IVF with multifetal pregnancy reduction. In this case, several fertilized eggs are implanted in a woman's womb, and after a certain period of time, the one or two unborn children that look the strongest and healthiest are allowed to survive, while the others are destroyed. This too is a form of abortion, and is not morally acceptable.

2. Artificial Insemination by Donor (AID). Artificial insemination with the sperm of a man who is not the husband is called artificial insemination by donor (abbreviated AID). While some ethicists believe this is morally acceptable in certain cases,[46] it does not seem so to me. It oversteps the boundaries of the pattern of laws that God established in Scripture, which always sought to guarantee that a child would be conceived by and born to a man and a woman who are married to each other (see discussion above,

---

46. See Feinberg and Feinberg, *Ethics for a Brave New World*, 405–6.

pp. 43–46). But in this case the child is conceived by a man and a woman who are not married to each other. While people might differ as to whether this technically constitutes adultery, it certainly is a transgression of the normal means by which God planned for children to be conceived and born.

In addition, there are some possible emotional complexities that, while not providing a direct scriptural argument against AID, still alert us to the danger of introducing significant stress into a marriage. If a woman receives artificial insemination from a man who is not her husband, she will go through the intensely personal and life-changing experience of carrying a child through pregnancy to birth without the deep satisfaction of knowing that the child inside her was conceived with her husband. It is not unreasonable to think that the mother will wonder what kind of man the (perhaps anonymous) sperm donor is, and if she ever might be able to meet him. Such emotional complexities will not be healthy for the marriage relationship. (I do not claim that such emotional temptations prove that this arrangement is morally unacceptable, but I simply mention here that AID can put more strain than is expected on a marriage relationship.)

The use of AID by a woman who has no husband is clearly morally unacceptable. This would include a single woman being impregnated from a sperm bank, thus violating God's intent that children should be conceived by and born to a man and a woman who are married to each other.

The moral laws that God gave in Scripture were designed to prevent unmarried women from conceiving children with men to whom they were not married, and thereby intentionally bearing children who would not have fathers to help raise them.[47]

Similarly, the use of AID by a woman in a lesbian relationship in order to bear a child is a violation of the principle that a child should be conceived by and born to a man and a woman who are married to each other, not two women who are living together.[48]

3. Surrogate Motherhood. Sometimes a married woman who is physically unable to carry and bear children herself will reach an agreement with another woman, who agrees to be impregnated with the original couple's embryo and carry the child to term. This could involve in vitro fertilization, using both the egg and the sperm of the married couple, or it could involve artificial insemination by donor, using the husband's sperm but the surrogate mother's egg.

This arrangement also seems to me to violate God's intention that children should be conceived by and born to a man and a woman who are married to each other. In this case the child would not be born to the woman who is part of the married couple, but to the surrogate mother.[49]

---

47. This is a different situation from a single man or woman adopting a child who has already been born or even adopting a frozen embryo; see the section on embryo adoption above, pp. 53–57.

48 See Grudem, *Christian Ethics*, 846–71, for a discussion of homosexuality.

49. Feinberg and Feinberg think that surrogate motherhood involving in vitro fertilization using the original couple's sperm and egg is morally acceptable in certain limited situations; see *Ethics for a Brave New World*, 442–43. They raise

In addition, the likely emotional components of this arrangement must be given serious consideration. It is likely that the personal intimacy involved in carrying and bearing a child will be so deep that the process of surrogate motherhood runs the danger of putting a nearly intolerable strain on the marriage. The husband and wife are including a third person into their marriage relationship, at least in some senses. The husband may find himself with an increasing emotional attachment to the woman who is bearing his child. The surrogate mother will likely feel a similar emotional attachment to the man whose child she is bearing. And the deep bond that inevitably develops between a woman and the child she bears will be disrupted and broken only with much heartache, and possibly even legal battles.

The most famous surrogacy case was perhaps the battle over "Baby M" in the mid-1980s. A surrogate (Mary Beth Whitehead) agreed to carry a child for Elizabeth and William Stern, using her own egg and artificial insemination with his sperm. But she then reneged on the agreement to give the Sterns the child. The New Jersey Supreme Court ruled that a mother could not be forced to surrender her child, and in 1988 declared Ms. Whitehead the legal

---

a very interesting but highly unusual possibility—early in a pregnancy the mother unexpectedly dies, and a friend or relative is willing to carry the baby to term so that the baby does not also die. They say that in such a case, "We think surrogacy would be moral" (443). I agree with them in this highly unusual case, for it would be similar to the case of adopting a frozen embryo, which I discussed above. But this does not provide an argument for the legitimacy of surrogacy in other situations, for in this highly unusual case there was no intention to involve surrogate motherhood at the time of the initial conception of the child.

mother. Because of that precedent, almost all surrogacy agreements are now gestational—using not the egg of the surrogate mother but the egg of the intended mother, or an anonymous egg from a donor.[50]

In 2012, the New Jersey Supreme Court tackled another surrogacy case in which a husband and wife obtained an egg from an anonymous donor and made an agreement with a surrogate mother to carry it for them. They had the surrogate renounce all legal rights to the child and had a judge preemptively put their names on the birth certificate. A hospital worker questioned this arrangement—a child born to one woman, but intended for another—and called the state bureau of vital statistics. The bureau called the attorney general's office, which sued to overturn the judge's order about the birth certificate. A lower court agreed with the attorney general and stripped the mother's name from the birth certificate. The New Jersey Supreme Court deadlocked on the issue. The court's split basically left the child legally motherless.[51]

There is one event in Scripture that bears several similarities to the modern practice of surrogate motherhood: Abram (later Abraham) conceived a child with Hagar, the Egyptian maidservant of his wife, Sarai (later Sarah). Almost immediately it led to marital conflict, and much strife followed:

50. Kate Zernike, "Court's Split Decision Provides Little Clarity on Surrogacy," *The New York Times*, Oct. 24, 2012, http://www.nytimes.com/2012/10/25/nyregion/in-surrogacy-case-nj-supreme-court-is-deadlocked-over-whom-to-call-mom.html.

51. Zernike, "Court's Split Decision Provides Little Clarity on Surrogacy."

Now Sarai, Abram's wife, had borne him no children. She had a female Egyptian servant whose name was Hagar. And Sarai said to Abram, "Behold now, the LORD has prevented me from bearing children. *Go in to my servant; it may be that I shall obtain children by her.*" And Abram listened to the voice of Sarai. So, after Abram had lived ten years in the land of Canaan, Sarai, Abram's wife, took Hagar the Egyptian, her servant, and gave her to Abram her husband as a wife. *And he went in to Hagar, and she conceived.* And when she saw that she had conceived, she looked with contempt on her mistress. And Sarai said to Abram, "May the wrong done to me be on you! I gave my servant to your embrace, and when she saw that she had conceived, she looked on me with contempt. May the LORD judge between you and me!" (Gen. 16:1–5)

This case is not exactly like modern surrogate motherhood, for sexual intercourse was involved, and the child was born only from Abram's sperm, not from Abram's sperm and Sarai's egg. But deep interpersonal tension and conflict is evident from this narrative. A perceptive interpreter of Scripture will observe this resultant conflict (and the conflict that lasts even to this day between the Jewish people, who are descended from Abram and Sarai, and the Arab people, who are descended from Abram and Hagar) and rightly conclude that in this text God intends to warn us that such a means of bringing children into the world is likely to lead to much trouble.

Infertility is a cause of deep sorrow, distress, and grief for many couples, and we must recognize that and show understanding and compassion for those who experience this grief. But this deep grief should not be counted as a valid reason to overstep the moral boundaries that God has set in his Word concerning the conception and bearing of children.

4. Cloning. It is not currently possible for infertile couples to gain a child by cloning. But should this ever become possible, would it be morally acceptable?

Modern scientific advances have now made it possible to clone plants. For instance, a wood-products company can plant an entire field with cloned trees, so that every tree has the same shape of branches in the same place on the tree, and every tree grows to an identical height. Cloning has also been used to preserve vanishing varieties of trees.[52] I see no moral objection to this process, and it can make agricultural land more productive and result in better quality crops (or trees). This seems to me to be a legitimate part of subduing the earth, according to Genesis 1:28.

Another possibility is the cloning not of plants but of animals. According to the National Human Genome Research Institute, the following animals have been cloned: cow, sheep, cat, deer, dog, horse, mule, ox, rabbit, and rat. A rhesus monkey has been cloned by embryo splitting.[53]

52. Denisa R. Superville, "Historic trees get a second shot at life with cloning efforts," Phys.org, June 6, 2013, http://phys.org/news/2013-06-historic-trees-shot-life-cloning.html.

53. "Cloning Fact Sheet," National Human Genome Research Institute, https://www.genome.gov/about-genomics/fact-sheets/Cloning-Fact-Sheet.

I am uncertain how we should evaluate the cloning of animals from a moral standpoint. It might be possible to make a distinction between higher forms of animals, such as mammals (perhaps those that appeared to have "the breath of life" in them, see Gen. 1:30), and lower, less complex animals. Higher forms of animals (such as dogs, cats, horses, and chimpanzees) often seem to have something akin to a human personality, and it is common for domestic animals to develop a genuine kind of friendship with their human companions. It remains to be seen whether higher forms of animal life can actually be cloned successfully, so that they survive more than a short period of time. The first cloned animal, a sheep named Dolly, was born in 1996. Dolly died prematurely at the age of six from joint and lung problems associated with old age. However, four clones from her same line have turned nine and are doing just fine.[54] Two years after Dolly was born, researchers in Japan cloned eight calves from a single cow, but only four survived.[55]

But regarding the cloning of human beings, I think Christians should have significant moral objections. Scientists might think that they can create the *exact duplicate* of a world champion athlete or a scientist with an incredibly high IQ, but it will simply not be the same person in any case. All of the life circumstances and experiences that a

---

54. Rachel Feltman, "Dolly the Sheep Died Young—But Her Clones Seem Perfectly Healthy As They Turn 9," *The Washington Post*, July 26, 2016, https://www.washingtonpost.com/news/speaking-of-science/wp/2016/07/26/dolly-the-sheep-died-young-but-her-clones-seem-perfectly-healthy-as-they-turn-9/.

55. "Cloning Fact Sheet."

person goes through from childhood to adulthood could never be the same. Sometimes people become stronger by overcoming hardships, but would people want cloned duplicates of themselves to experience such hardships?

In addition, the process of producing a human being from cloning (if it could ever be done) is significantly different from God's intention that the wonderful diversity and variety of the human race be protected with children being born from a mixture of genetic information from both the father and the mother. This does not happen in cloning. God, in his wisdom, makes us all different as individuals, not as clones of one another, and in this way protects the uniqueness and value of each human being.

Moreover, there is a significant question as to whether a cloned human being, even if *physically* and *genetically* identical to the person from whose cells the cloning originated, would really be a human person at all. How would we know if this "person" even had a soul? Would God be forced by the cloning process to impart a human soul to a living creature that just happened to have a physical human body?

Scripture repeatedly speaks of our soul (or spirit) as something distinct from our physical bodies. When Rachel died, "*her soul was departing* (for she was dying)" (Gen. 35:18), and when Elijah prayed for a dead child to come back to life, he prayed that the child's "soul" would come into him again (1 Kings 17:21 RSV, KJV, NKJV[56]). Else-

---

56. Several translations render the Hebrew word *nephesh* as "life" in this verse (see ESV, NIV, NASB). The word can mean either "soul" or "life," depending on context. Ludwig Koehler and Walter Baumgartner, *The Hebrew and Aramaic Lexi-*

where the Old Testament speaks of death as a time when "the *spirit* returns to God who gave it" (Eccles. 12:7; see also Luke 23:46; John 19:30; Acts 7:59). And Scripture warns us that the origin of the connection between a person's body and spirit is mysterious, something that God does not reveal to us: "As you do not know the way the spirit comes to the bones in the womb of a woman with child, so you do not know the work of God who makes everything" (Eccles. 11:5).

But if our modern society begins to create physical human bodies without the sanction or blessing of God himself in the process, what will we in fact be creating? Could a human being without a soul even live at all? Or if so, would it have any conscience, any sense of right and wrong? These are deeply troubling questions.

Finally, the process of producing a cloned human being, even if it is possible, would once again violate the principle that God intends children to be conceived by and born to a man and woman who are married to each other, for a person who is cloned from one specific human being would not be created from a father and a mother who are married to each other. I conclude that cloning of human beings is morally unacceptable.

---

con of the Old Testament, study edition, 2 vols. (Leiden: Brill, 2001), 1.712–13; Francis Brown, S. R. Driver, and Charles Briggs, *A Hebrew and English Lexicon of the Old Testament* (Oxford: Clarendon, 1968), 659.

PART 3: ADOPTION

Adoption is often a wonderful option for childless couples, if it is their desire to be parents and something they believe God is calling them to do. Adoption is also a wonderful reflection of God's own actions in adopting us to be his children (see John 1:12; Rom. 8:14–17; Gal. 4:5; Eph. 1:5).[57] And adoption is a very practical way to care for "orphans," which is something that James says is part of "religion that is pure and undefiled before God the Father" (James 1:27). For these reasons, not only many childless couples but also many Christian couples who already have some naturally born children have decided that God is calling them to adopt one or more additional children. Russell Moore's 2009 book *Adopted for Life*[58] has had wide influence in promoting adoption among evangelical families.

Because Scripture views adoption in such a positive way, and because the adoption process is often difficult and expensive, some churches have established or work closely with programs that will provide financial, legal, and other support to couples as they go through the adoption process. For example, Bethlehem Baptist Church in Minneapolis partners with the "LYDIA Fund," which provides financial help for qualified Christian parents to adopt children from orphanages around the world.[59] Focus on the Family offers

---

57. See Grudem, *Systematic Theology*, 736–45.
58. Russell D. Moore, *Adopted for Life: The Priority of Adoption for Christian Families and Churches* (Wheaton, IL: Crossway, 2009).
59. See "Adoption," Bethlehem Baptist Church, https://bethlehem.church /adoption/.

a number of resources to help parents seeking to adopt children.[60] And Bethany Christian Services is another organization that provides a wide range of assistance to couples seeking to adopt,[61] as do numerous other state and local adoption ministries.

60. See Debi Grebenik, "Characteristics of Successful Adoptive Families," Focus on the Family, Jan. 1, 2008, http://www.focusonthefamily.com/parenting/adoptive-families/.

61. See "Your Adoption Journey Begins Here," Bethany Christian Services, https://www.bethany.org/adoption.

FURTHER RESOURCES

QUESTIONS FOR PERSONAL APPLICATION

1. Do you tend to view children more as a burden or as a positive blessing?

2. Consider the possibility that you will have several children (say, five, six, or more). If that happened, do you think they would bring mostly positive or mostly negative consequences to the world in the future? Does the idea of having that many children cause you to fear that you might not be able to afford it or that you might not be able to be a good enough parent? How do you think God would view this possibility?

3. What do you think would be the ideal number of children for you to have?

4. What character traits will help to influence you to have the right attitudes and make the right decisions regarding birth control?

5. If you are unable to have children because of some kind of infertility, how fully would you say you are trusting God to bring good out of this situation, in the sense of Romans 8:28? To what extent has God given your heart peace about this matter?

6. Considering the various kinds of modern reproductive technology discussed in this book, which of them would you be comfortable using in your own marriage if you faced a situation of infertility?

Which of them would you not think appropriate for you, or not morally acceptable?

7. What do you think about the idea of embryo adoption? Do you think churches should promote this idea more actively?

8. Do you think it would be morally right for scientists to attempt to clone a human being? Do you think there should be laws prohibiting this?

9. Do you know friends or relatives who have adopted one or more children? Would you say their overall experience has been positive or negative? If it has been a positive experience, what factors contributed to this?

SPECIAL TERMS

abortifacient
artificial insemination by donor (AID)
artificial insemination by husband (AIH)
cloning
cryopreservation
embryo adoption
infertility
IUD
in vitro fertilization (IVF)
natural family planning (NFP)
prefertilization genetic screening
rhythm method
RU-486
snowflake children
surrogate motherhood

BIBLIOGRAPHY

Sections in Christian Ethics Texts

Clark, David K., and Robert V. Rakestraw, eds. *Readings in Christian Ethics*. 2 vols. Grand Rapids, MI: Baker, 1994, 2:57–94.

Davis, John Jefferson. *Evangelical Ethics: Issues Facing the Church Today*. 4th ed. Phillipsburg, NJ: P&R, 2015, 17–89.

Feinberg, John S., and Paul D. Feinberg. *Ethics for a Brave New World*. 2nd ed. Wheaton, IL: Crossway, 2010, 286–306, 387–459.

Frame, John M. *The Doctrine of the Christian Life: A Theology of Lordship*. Phillipsburg, NJ: P&R, 2008, 782–95.

Geisler, Norman L. *Christian Ethics: Contemporary Issues and Options*. 2nd ed. Grand Rapids, MI: Baker, 2010, 180–98, 396–405.

Gushee, David P., and Glen H. Stassen. *Kingdom Ethics: Following Jesus in Contemporary Context*. 2nd ed. Grand Rapids, MI: Eerdmans, 2016, 428–34.

Kaiser, Walter C., Jr. *What Does the Lord Require? A Guide for Preaching and Teaching Biblical Ethics*. Grand Rapids, MI: Baker, 2009, 151–62.

McQuilkin, Robertson, and Paul Copan. *An Introduction to Biblical Ethics: Walking in the Way of Wisdom*. 3rd ed. Downers Grove, IL: InterVarsity Press, 2014, 333–34, 396–99.

Murray, John. *Principles of Conduct: Aspects of Biblical Ethics*. 3rd ed. Grand Rapids, MI: Zondervan, 2009, 45–81.

Rae, Scott B. *Moral Choices: An Introduction to Ethics*. 3rd ed. Grand Rapids, MI: Zondervan, 2009, 155–81, 286–89.

Other Works

Atkinson, David J., and David H. Field, eds. *New Dictionary of Christian Ethics and Pastoral Theology*. Leicester, UK: Inter-Varsity, and Downers Grove, IL: InterVarsity Press, 1995.

Batura, Paul J., Eric Metaxas, and Larry King. *Chosen for Greatness: How Adoption Changes the World*. Washington, DC: Regnery Faith, 2016.

Best, Megan. *Fearfully and Wonderfully Made: Ethics and the Beginning of Human Life*. Kingsford, NSW, Australia: Matthias Media, 2012.

Biebel, David B., ed. *The Sterilization Option: A Guide for Christians*. Grand Rapids, MI: Baker, 1995.

Brinton, Sara, and Amanda Bennett. *In Defense of the Fatherless: Redeeming International Adoption & Orphan Care*. Fearn, Ross-shire, Scotland: Christian Focus, 2015.

Cook, E. David. "Reproductive Technologies." In *Dictionary of Scripture and Ethics*, edited by Joel B. Green, 669–71. Grand Rapids, MI: Baker, 2011.

Cutrer, William R., and Sandra L. Glahn. *The Contraception Guidebook: Options, Risks, and Answers for Christian Couples*. Grand Rapids, MI: Zondervan, 2005.

Doriani, Daniel. "Birth Dearth or Bring on the Babies? Biblical Perspectives on Family-Planning." *Journal of Biblical Counseling* 12, no. 1 (1993): 24–35.

Fletcher, D. B. "Birth Control." In *New Dictionary of Christian Ethics and Pastoral Theology*, 193–95.

Fletcher, D. B. "Reproductive Technologies." In *New Dictionary of Christian Ethics and Pastoral Theology*, 733–34.

Hui, Edwin C. *At the Beginning of Life: Dilemmas in Theological Bioethics*. Downers Grove, IL: InterVarsity Press, 2002.

Kilner, John F. *Dignity and Destiny: Humanity in the Image of God*. Grand Rapids, MI: Eerdmans, 2015.

Kilner, John F., ed. *Why the Church Needs Bioethics: A Guide to Wise Engagement with Life's Challenges*. Grand Rapids, MI: Zondervan, 2011.

Kilner, John Frederic, and C. Ben Mitchell. *Does God Need Our Help? Cloning, Assisted Suicide, and Other Challenges in Bioethics*. Vital Questions. Wheaton, IL: Tyndale, 2003.

Köstenberger, Andreas J. "To Have or Not to Have Children: Special Issues Related to the Family, Part 1." In *God, Marriage, and Family: Rebuilding the Biblical Foundation*, 2nd ed., 117–37, 334–40. Wheaton, IL: Crossway, 2010

Meilaender, Gilbert. *Not by Nature but by Grace: Forming Families through Adoption*. Notre Dame, IN: University of Notre Dame Press, 2016.

Mitchell, C. Ben. *Biotechnology and the Human Good*. Washington, DC: Georgetown University Press, 2007.

Mitchell, C. Ben, and D. Joy Riley. *Christian Bioethics: A Guide for Pastors, Health Care Professionals, and Families*. B&H Studies in Christian Ethics. Nashville: B&H Academic, 2014.

Moore, Russell D. *Adopted for Life: The Priority of Adoption for Christian Families and Churches*. Wheaton, IL: Crossway, 2009.

Moore, Russell D. *Adoption: What Joseph of Nazareth Can Teach Us about This Countercultural Choice*. Wheaton, IL: Crossway, 2015.

Moore, Russell, Andrew T. Walker, and Randy Stinson. *The Gospel & Adoption*. Nashville: B&H, 2017.

Pride, Mary. *The Way Home: Beyond Feminism, Back to Reality*. Westchester, IL: Crossway, 1985.

Rae, Scott B. *Brave New Families: Biblical Ethics and Reproductive Technologies*. Grand Rapids, MI: Baker, 1996.

Rae, Scott B. *Outside the Womb: Moral Guidance for Assisted Reproduction*. Chicago: Moody, 2011.

VanDrunen, David. *Bioethics and the Christian Life: A Guide to Making Difficult Decisions*. Wheaton, IL: Crossway, 2009.

Wheat, Ed, and Gaye Wheat. *Intended for Pleasure: Sex Technique and Sexual Fulfillment in Christian Marriage*, 4th ed., 162–94. Grand Rapids, MI: Revell, 2010.

SCRIPTURE MEMORY PASSAGES

Psalm 127:3: Behold, children are a heritage from the Lord, the fruit of the womb a reward.

1 Peter 1:6–7: In this you rejoice, though now for a little while, if necessary, you have been grieved by various trials, so that the tested genuineness of your faith—more precious than gold that perishes though it is tested by fire—may be found to result in praise and glory and honor at the revelation of Jesus Christ.

HYMNS

"All the Way My Savior Leads Me"

All the way my Savior leads me—What have I to ask
   beside?

Can I doubt His tender mercy, who thru life has been
    my Guide?
Heav'nly peace, divinest comfort, here by faith in
    Him to dwell!
For I know, whate'er befall me, Jesus doeth all
    things well.

All the way my Savior leads me—Cheers each
    winding path I tread,
Gives me grace for ev'ry trial, feeds me with the
    living bread.
Tho my weary steps may falter and my soul athirst
    may be,
Gushing from the Rock before me, lo! a spring of joy
    I see.

All the way my Savior leads me—O the fullness of
    His love!
Perfect rest to me is promised in my Father's house
    above.
When my spirit, clothed immortal, wings its flight to
    realms of day,
This my song thru endless ages: Jesus led me all
    the way.

                              Fanny J. Crosby, 1820–1915

"It Is Well with My Soul"

When peace, like a river, attendeth my way,
When sorrows like sea billows roll;
Whatever my lot, Thou hast taught me to say,
"It is well, it is well with my soul."

Refrain:
It is well
With my soul,
It is well, it is well
With my soul.

Tho Satan should buffet, tho trials should come,
Let this blest assurance control,
That Christ hath regarded my helpless estate,
And hath shed His own blood for my soul.

My sin—O the bliss of this glorious tho't
My sin, not in part, but the whole,
Is nailed to the cross, and I bear it no more:
Praise the Lord, praise the Lord, O my soul!

And, Lord, haste the day when my faith shall be sight,
The clouds be rolled back as a scroll:
The trump shall resound and the Lord shall descend,
Even so, it is well with my soul.

Horatio G. Spafford, 1828–1888

Scripture Versions Cited

General Index

abortifacients, 23
abortion, 23–24, 60
Abraham, 25, 37, 64–65
Absalom, 16
Adam, 13, 18, 31–33, 38, 41, 44
adoption, 53–57, 70–71
adultery, 44
animals, 66–67
artificial insemination by donor
    (AID), 60–62
artificial insemination by hus-
    band (AIH), 47
assisted reproductive technology
    (ART), 46

"Baby M," 63
barrenness, 25, 37, 38, 40
Bethany Christian Services, 71
Bethlehem Baptist Church
    (Minneapolis), 70
birth control
  as morally acceptable, 20–24
  Scripture on, 11–20
  as wrong, 25–34
birth-control pills, 22

calling, 27–28, 36
Canada, 18
Chadwick, Jacque, 59n45

character traits, 72
childbirth, 32–33
children, as blessing, 12–17,
    26–28, 34–36, 38, 72
China, 19
chlamydia, 57
church, expansion of, 15–16
cloning, 66–69
college, 12–13
conception, 23, 42–43, 52n32
condoms, 11, 22
creation mandate, 13, 18,
    31–32, 41–42, 44, 66
cryopreservation, 50
Cunningham, Paige Comstock,
    58n44
cystic fibrosis, 57

David, 16, 42–43
death, 69
diaphragm, 22
disability, 15n7, 32, 38, 42, 49
disease, 38, 42, 57–58
Dolly (sheep), 67
Doriani, Daniel, 30

education, 20
Elijah, 68
Elizabeth, 37, 39–40, 43

Elkanah, 24
ellaOne, 23
embryo adoption, 53–57
embryos, freezing of, 50
emotional complexities, 61, 63
erectile dysfunction, 49
Esau, 43
eugenics, 58n44, 60
evangelical Christians, 48
Eve, 13, 18, 31–33, 38, 41, 44

faith, 39–40
fall, 31–33, 38
fatherless, 55n38
fear, 36
Feinberg, John S., 21, 46n28,
    51, 55n39, 62n49
Feinberg, Paul D., 21, 46n28,
    51, 55n39, 62n49
fertility, 32–33
fertility rates, 18–19
financial stability, 20
Focus on the Family, 70–71
food, 26
fornication, 45
Frame, John M., 46n28
freedom, 27–28
frozen embryos, 50

genetic screening, 57–58, 59
Germany, 19
God, sovereignty of, 28–30
gonorrhea, 57
grief, 38–39, 66

Hagar, 64–65
Hannah, 24, 37, 38
happiness, 12
Harrison, Donna, 23–24

heart malformation, 57
hemophilia, 57
homosexuality, 62
human agency, 28–30
Hungary, 18
Huntington's disease, 57

illness, 32
image of God, 58
India, 19
infertility, 24, 37–41, 42, 47,
    48, 66
intrauterine device (IUD),
    23–24
in vitro fertilization (IVF),
    48–53, 59–60
Italy, 18

Jacob, 24, 37, 43
Jade, Marley, 55–56
Japan, 18, 19
Jesus Christ
    on children, 14
    on divorce, 45
    virgin birth of, 44n27
John the Baptist, 37

Kilner, John F., 46n28
kingdom of God, expansion of,
    15–16

Lawlor, Debbie, 50
lesbianism, 62
Life Issues Institute, 22
LYDIA Fund, 70

Mark, 41
marriage
    and conception, 43–46, 47,
        60–62, 69

sexual intimacy in, 34
strain on, 63
Massachusetts, 19
medicine, 41, 47
Mitchell, C. Ben, 46n28
Moore, Russell, 70
morning-after pills, 23

National Human Genome
Research Institute, 66–67
natural, 48
natural family planning (NFP),
22, 25
natural law, 31
Netherlands, 19
new covenant age, 15
New Jersey Supreme Court,
63–64
New Testament, on spiritual
children, 41
non-Christian culture, 36

"one flesh," 34, 52n32
orphans, 54–55, 70
overpopulation, 17–20

Paul, 15, 27, 40, 41
plants, 66
porneia, 45
prefertilization genetic screening, 57–58
preimplantation genetic diagnosis
(PGD), 59
Pride, Mary, 26, 27, 28
procreation, 34
prosperity, 18, 19
Protestants, 12

Rachel, 24, 37, 38, 68
Rae, Scott B., 46n28

Rebekah, 43
reproductive technology, moral-
ity of, 41–58
responsibility, 20–21
rhythm method, 22
Roman Catholic Church,
11–12, 23n18, 31
RU-486, 23
Russia, 18

Samson, 37
Sarah, 37, 64–65
secondary means, 28–30
selfishness, 36
sexual immorality, 45
sexual intercourse, 33–34, 44
sexually transmitted diseases,
57
single-parent households, 56–57
sleep, 26
"snowflake children," 54
Society of Assisted Reproductive
Technologies (SART), 53
sorrow, 16, 39–40
soul, 68–69
South Korea, 18
spermicide, 22
spirit, 68–69
spiritual children, 15, 41
sponge, 22
Stern, Elizabeth, 63
Stern, William, 63
Strege, Hannah, 55
suffering, 40
surrogate motherhood, 62–66
syphilis, 57

thermometer, 48–49
Timothy, 41

Titus, 41
trials, 40
Trinity Evangelical Divinity
      School, 51
trust, in God, 28–30
tubal ligation, 23

unborn children, 42–43, 47
United Kingdom, 19
unwanted pregnancy, 11

VanDrunen, David, 46n28
vasectomy, 23
Viagra, 49
virgin birth, 44n27

Whitehead, Mary Beth, 63
widows, 15
wisdom, 35
work, 26

Zechariah, 37, 39–40

Scripture Index

Genesis
1:28 . . . . .13, 18, 31,
35, 38, 41,
44
1:30 67
1:31 20
2:24 . . . . .34, 44
2:25 44
3:16 32
3:17–18 31
11:30 37
15:3 25
16:1 37
16:1–5 65
21:1–7 37
25:22–23 43
29:31 37
30:1 . . . . .24, 38
35:18 68

Exodus
20:14 44
21:22–25 43
22:16 45
22:17 45
22:22 . . . . .55n38
23:26 38

Leviticus
20:10 44

Deuteronomy
5:18 44
7:14 38
10:18 . . . . .55n38
21:18–21 17
22:28–29 45
24:17 . . . . .55n38
24:19–21 . . . . .55n38
26:12–13 . . . . .55n38
27:19 . . . . .55n38

Judges
13:2 37

1 Samuel
1:2–18 37
1:5–10 38
1:8 24
1:10 24

2 Samuel
13–18 16

1 Kings
17:21 68

Psalms
10:14...............55n38
10:18...............55n38
24:1................42
51:5................23, 43
68:5................55n38
82:3................55n38
113:9...............25, 38
127:2...............26
127:3...............38, 77
127:3–5............14, 35
128:3–4............14, 35, 38
139:13.............43
146:9..............55n38

Proverbs
5:18–19............34
6:10–11............26
6:32................44
10:1................16
17:25...............17
19:13...............17
29:3................17

Ecclesiastes
2:24................26
3:13................26
5:18................26
11:5................69
12:7................69

Isaiah
1:17................55n38
45:18..............20
54:1................25, 38

Jeremiah
7:6.................55n38
22:3................55n38

Hosea
14:3 55

Zechariah
7:10 ....55n38

Malachi
2:15 ....14, 35, 38
4:5–6..............17

Matthew
15:19..............44
19:6 45
19:13–15 14

Luke
1:5–7..............39–40
1:6.................39
1:7.................37
1:44 43
1:57–66............37
4:40 42
14:28..............21, 35
15:11–32 16
23:46..............69

John
1:12 70
19:30..............69

Acts
7:59 69

Romans
8:14–17............70
8:28 72
13:9 44
14:4 36
14:10..............36

1 Corinthians
4:15 41
6:18 45
7:7 36
7:17 27
12:20 28

2 Corinthians
12:21 45

Galatians
4:5 70
4:19 41
4:27 38
5:19 45

Ephesians
1:5 70
5:3 45
5:31 34
6:4 22

Colossians
3:5 45

1 Thessalonians
4:3 45

1 Timothy
1:2 41
5:8 ....21, 35
5:14 ....15, 35, 38

Titus
1:4 41

James
1:2–4 40
1:5–6 35
1:27 ....55, 70
2:11 44

1 Peter
1:6–7 77
1:6–9 40
5:13 41

2 Peter
2:14 44

Also Available from Wayne Grudem

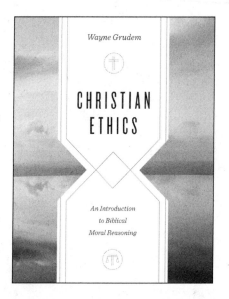

In this comprehensive volume on Christian ethics, best-selling author Wayne Grudem explains in detail what the whole Bible says about living as a Christian.

"Insightful, encyclopedic, biblical, and distinctively evangelical, this book from Wayne Grudem is a massive contribution to Christian ethics."
R. ALBERT MOHLER JR.

For more information, visit **crossway.org**.

Accessible Booklets Answering Complex Ethical Questions